MW01206207

Witcheficent's

BAT STEW

by Dan G.

Every Friday 13th
at a quarter past two,

Witcheficent makes
her most famous bat stew.

So if you are silly,
then you can brew, too.

Just follow the formula
of you-know-who.

She starts with ONE cauldron
and fills it with goo.

Adds spices, like garlic,
and an old rubber shoe.

She then clips the nails
from the paws of TWO shrew.

(It's a secret ingredient
from Aunt Whoop-de-doo)

She throws in THREE bat eggs
(she stole from the zoo)

She melts pounds of lard
from FOUR fat caribou.

To boil, with bat powder
for a screaming good roux.

She stirs counter-clock wise,
(this thickens the brew)

And she uses the end
of a broom she once flew.

She plops in FIVE onions
from her garden she grew.

Surprise! Yes, she gardens.
What's the hullabaloo?

She simmers SIX bat eyes,
that are easy to chew.
Which she does 'cause she likes
to play bat peek-a-boo.

EIGHT cups of milk,
Squeezed from a zebu.

Conversion Chart

Cups	Gallons
1 cup	1/16 gal
8 cups	1/2 gal

Will give the concoction
it's gross greenish hue.

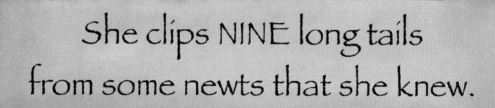

She clips NINE long tails
from some newts that she knew.

NEWTS
1. Larry ——— green
2. Petunia ——— yellow
3. Scary Joe ——— brown
4. Neville ——— albino
5. Mom ——— black-ish
6. Yannick ——— red
7. Bob ——— blue
8. Crystal ——— orange
9. Eileen ——— violet

Don't worry, these tails
are just tails that regrew.

Then ELEVEN warm toadstools
she's grown from mildew.

and if she can't find them,
she'll use old tofu.

When the moment's just right,
she will use ju-jitsu

to dig up TWELVE worms.
Then... she just might be through!

While Witcheficent grabs
her big spoon of bamboo,
We'll pause here a moment
so you won't misconstrue
Don't try this at home,
that would be a miscue.
You shouldn't eat bats.
That is simply cuckoo.

Kook
who?

So next time you're offered
a big bowl of bat stew,

Scare Witcheficent off
by telling her....

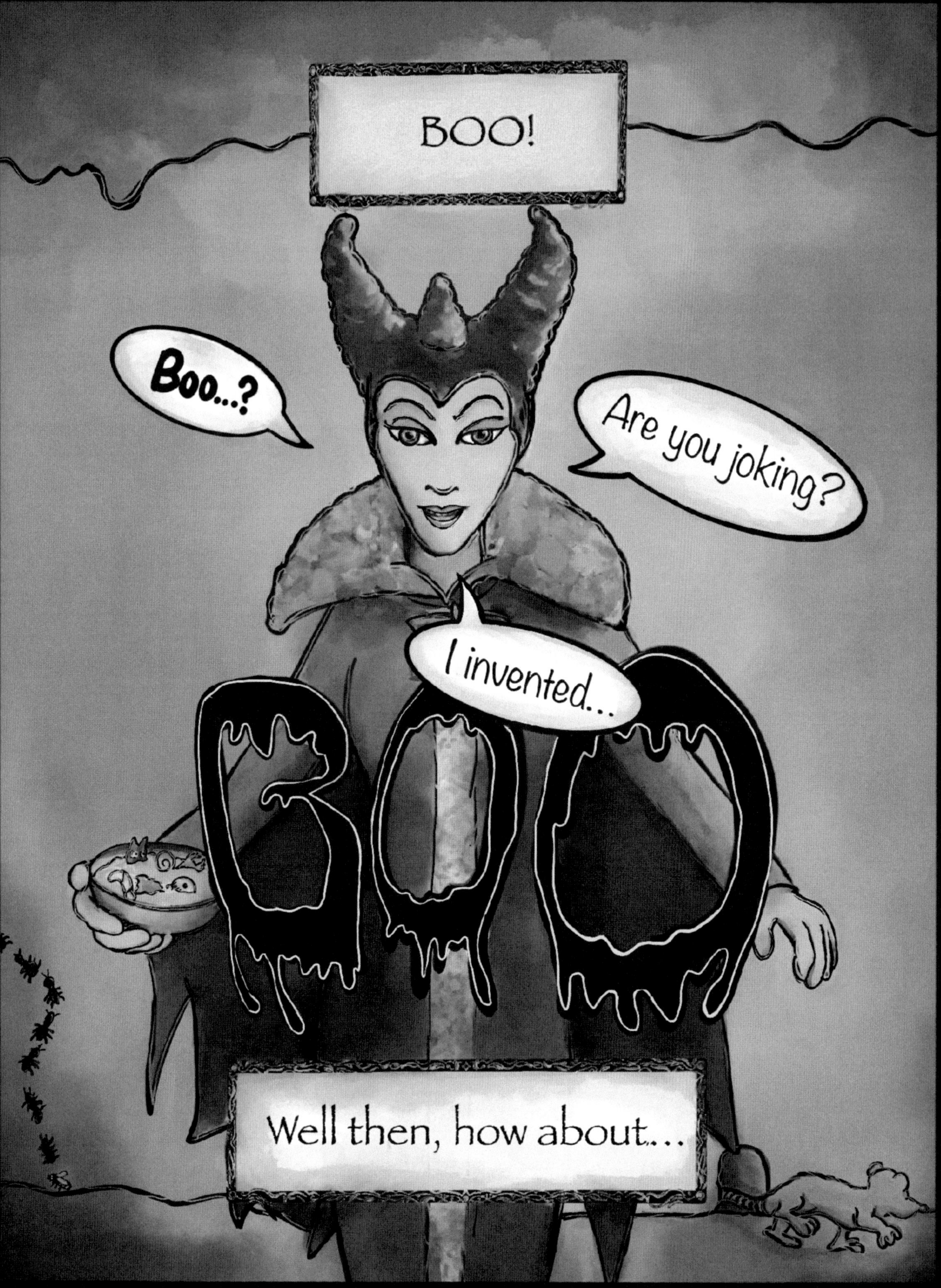
BOO!
Boo...?
Are you joking?
I invented...
BOO
Well then, how about...

List of Ingredients

1.
2.
3.
4.
5.
6.
7.
8.
9.
10.
11.
12.
13.

How to Draw Witcheficent

triangles

1. Use pencil To lightly *Sketch SHAPES

Oval →

half-Oval ← (for the collar)

2. Divide face in halves, up and down and sideways

3. make small marks inbetween outside edge and midlines

Straight lines for neck

4. sketch in curvy lines for her horns

5. add curves for helmet head

6. draw small circles above the mid-lines for irises

7. add three curvy lines above, below and midway through the circles

8. draw curvy lines for lips at midline

then, Erase lines and top of Circle

9. Small curve for nose at midline

10. Sketch in: bat necklace, and shoulders.

curvy collar,

*DON'T sketch DARK at first (So you can erase lines later)

11. Erase sketch lines from face head and body.

12. Sketch in curvy eyebrows

13. add small half circles for pupils

14. small upwards lines on sides of nose

15. Darken in helmet and horns

Keep white (don't fill in) for affect of reflected light

Darken on one side for **Shadow**

create ridges

and erase this

16. Give her a long "witchy" chin with this shape

17. Lastly Darken in and add details

lighty darken eyelids

Such as shadowing fun squiggles

add your signature →

Want more help? Then WATCH This ⅁

Other Titles
By Dan G.

Available at amazon.com

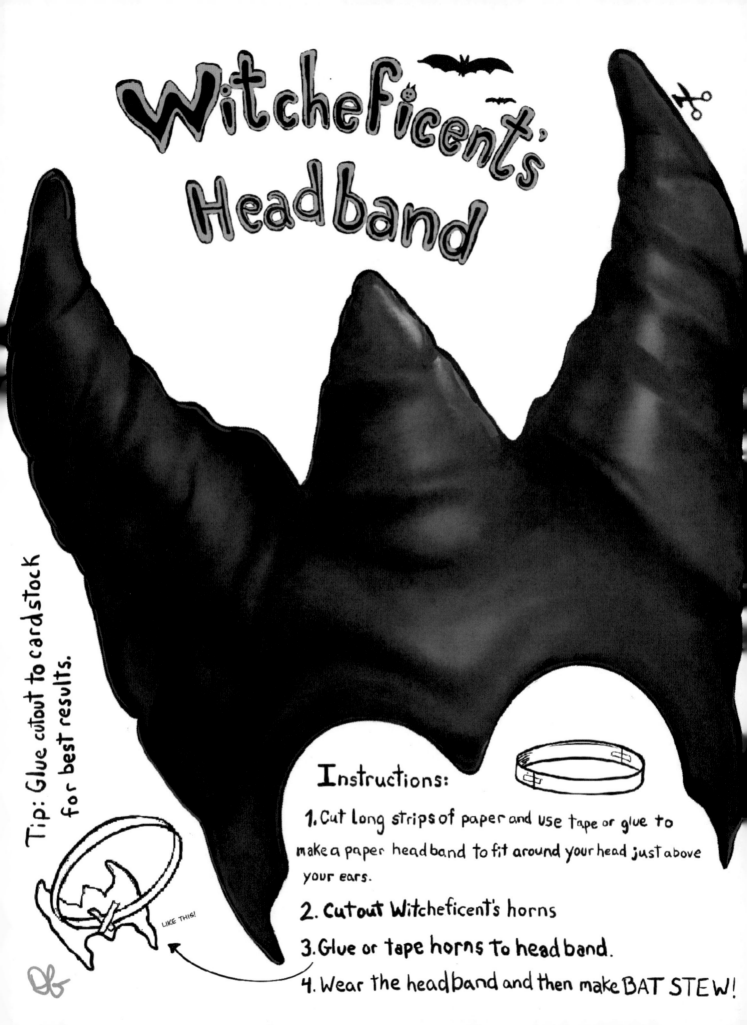

Witcheficent's Headband

Tip: Glue cutout to cardstock for best results.

LIKE THIS!

Instructions:

1. Cut long strips of paper and use tape or glue to make a paper headband to fit around your head just above your ears.

2. Cutout Witcheficent's horns

3. Glue or tape horns to headband.

4. Wear the headband and then make BAT STEW!